Creativity:

An Essential Tool for the Real World

By Mary Beth Magee

Published by BOTR Press, LLC

Poplarville, MS

All rights reserved. No part of this book may be used or reproduced by any means, graphic, electronic or mechanical, including photocopying, recording, taping or by any information storage electrical system without the written permission of the author except in the case of brief quotations embodied in critical articles and review.

Copyright 2021   Mary Beth Magee
Published by BOTR Press, LLC
www.BOTRPress.com

Cover photograph by Armand Khoury
Graphics by Mary Beth Magee

This is an original work based on the author's research and personal experience.

Creativity:

An Essential Tool for the Real World

By Mary Beth Magee

Dedicated to the creative spark inside each of us. May we let it take hold and burn so brightly it lights the world!

Contents

Forward 1

Introduction 5

What is Creativity? 6

A Formula for Creativity 9

Inspiration 10

    Sources of Inspiration 11

    Collect things 11

    Photograph places, people and things. 15

    Copy things 18

    Study things 21

    Listen to inspiring music 23

Imagination 25

    Read 27

    Visit 30

    Attend 32

    Borrow from the Arts 34

    Observe 37

    Play a game 40

    "What If?" the Situation 43

    Laugh often. 46

Information 49

    Reading 49

    Experience your world 51

Write it down	53
Record your idea fragments	55
Start Creating	57
Appendix	59
The Creativity Bill of Rights	60
A Few Suggested Games	61
Creativity Exercises	62
Some Suggested Reading	63
To Hercules	64
Photo Credits	65
Books by Mary Beth Magee	66
Connect with Mary Beth Magee	68
Where to Find Books by Mary Beth Magee	69
End Notes	70

Forward

The term "creativity" is often reserved almost exclusively to the arts—music, writing, dance, painting, etc.—but in fact creativity happens whenever people look at the world around them and ask that age-old question: "What if?" The human race has been asking this question since the world began, and it has taken us far:

- "What if Pythagoras and Aristotle were right, and the world *is* round? Couldn't we reach China by sailing west instead of East?

- "What if we were to build a bridge that floats on the water rather than rises above it, so it won't matter how deep the water is or how soft the seabed?"

- "What if we could harness the energy in the atom so we could utilize its power?"

- "What if we could fly high enough to leave the Earth's atmosphere? How much farther might we go?

I contend that every invention in the history of the world is the fruit born from combining something observed and the "What if?" with a healthy dose of creative imagination.

The answer to the "What if?" might be as complex as discovering a new vaccine or as simple as rearranging the furniture in a classroom to facilitate class discussions. The key is in the "What if?" because once you ask that question, your brain automatically starts to weigh the possibilities.

Hence, we have gone from the Nautilus of Jules Verne's fictional account of *20,000 Leagues Under the Sea* to modern nuclear-powered submarines that can stay under water for ninety days at a time; from *Star Trek's* 1960's Hollywood communicators to real life, world-wide cellular communication.

I contend that if observation—either through firsthand experience or through reading—is the seed, then the "What if" is the act of planting the seed to reveal the potential life inside. It takes a lot of imagination to envision the tree that might grow from that tiny seed, not to mention a lot of information on how to nurture that seed with the right amount of water and nutrition, so it will grow into a healthy tree. Put it all together, and something creative will grow out of that simple act of asking, "What if I put this seed into this soil then feed and water it in this way?"

What makes the potential possible, of course, is the one other magical ingredient that proves second nature to children everywhere, though I have known some adults who have, sadly, lost it: curiosity. If we can nurture curiosity, this essential part of human nature, in our children—and in ourselves—the resulting life-long learning can lead to creativity that can, indeed, take us far.

In *Creativity: An Essential Tool for the Real World* Mary Beth Magee explores the concepts of inspiration and imagination as they come together in this phenomenon we call creativity. Youngsters have an untapped potential for creativity, and we can help them to explore and expand it to the fullest by encouraging them to ask, "What if?"

Laura Anne Ewald
Picayune, MS

Introduction

Each of us sees the world through a different lens. Your past experiences, education, personality and cultural background help to form the lens. As you deal with the world on a day-to-day basis, your perspective grows and changes. Your needs change. How do you meet those needs?

When you engage the tools of your mind and experiences to solve problems and meet needs, you utilize creativity.

For example, a teacher puts together a lesson plan to involve students in the learning process. A businessman calculates a strategy for overcoming a supply chain problem. An inventor works on a new product to meet a societal need. A doctor works on a new treatment protocol for an illness. Each of them puts creativity to work.

In the pages of this book, you will find suggestions, techniques and exercises to help you connect to your creativity and find innovative solutions to the situations you encounter. I will give you examples of some of the ways I keep my own creativity flowing, in the hope you will find your own tools and processes.

Creativity easily could form the subject of a lifelong intellectual pursuit. A starting point for the first leg of the journey awaits you just ahead.

What is Creativity?

Ask any group of people to define creativity and you will probably get as many different answers as there are people in the group. Everyone seems to have a very personal idea about creativity. In its most strict definition, creativity is nothing more complicated than "the ability to create."[i] Scientists and behaviorists go a bit farther.

> "…creativity is a multidimensional domain that could be executed in the arts, science, stage performance, the commercial enterprise and business innovation (Sawyer, 2006). Following Baas et al. (2015) who defined the roots of creative cognition in the arts and sciences, creativity is not just a cultural or social construct. Instead, it is an essential psychological and cognitive process as well (Csikszentmihalyi, 1999; Sawyer, 2006; Kaufman, 2009; Gaut, 2010; Perlovsky and Levine, 2012)."[ii]

Take a handful of ingredients from the refrigerator and pantry. Put them together in a scrumptious dish and serve it. The result comes from creativity at work. Great chefs use it all the time.

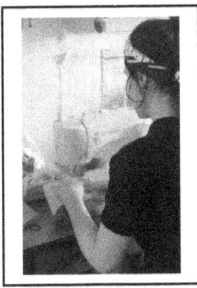

Look at a piece of fabric. Cut it out, sew it and embellish it. Wear the garment. Creativity strikes again, the same creativity used by the world's most famous designers.

Stand before a load which needs to be moved. Look at the equipment at hand. Put the pieces of equipment together in a combination to handle the load.

Study a task and choose the tools needed to complete it. Apply the tools to the project and enjoy the result.

Creativity has solved the problem. This aspect of problem-solving with creativity has taken humanity from caves to palaces.

So, why do we get so hung up on creativity?

Over the years, common usage of "creativity" has come to refer most often to the arts. Being creative has come to be synonymous with being artistic. If a person cannot draw or paint, cannot write or rhyme, they may be written off as "not creative." Not so. Creativity takes so many more forms than just the arts.

I hope, as you go through this book, you will see the many ways creativity can be expressed, not only in the arts, but also in the practical world and in our minds. You will learn ways to nurture and use your own creativity to make the world a better place.

A Formula for Creativity

Creativity does not take place in a vacuum. I believe a distinct formula or recipe comes into play. Although the recipe is particular in its format, it is chaotic in its implementation. Start with the basic components and follow your own instincts and interests to complete the process.

INSPIRATION

+ IMAGINATION

<u>+ INFORMATION</u>

CREATIVITY

Put the ingredients of the recipe together and creativity happens. The proportions, like any good recipe, may vary. The result may take many different forms. Yet each will be a sample of creativity at work.

Take a look at each of these ingredients. See how they contribute to the finished product.

Inspiration

Remember your last "Aha!" moment, the instant you saw a new path or identified the source of a problem? That instant marks inspiration at work. Think of inspiration as the heart of creativity.

Inspiration comes from within. Your heart, your mind, and your processing of the facts lead to inspiration. It comes from a place deep inside where all of the "stuff" you have taken into your brain gets whirled together like ingredients in a cerebral blender. What comes out is the ultimate creative smoothie!

Children are real pros at this process. Give them a big empty cardboard box, and they are inspired to become pirate captains or astronauts or part of a beleaguered garrison or…you get the idea. A blanket becomes a tent or a sail or a hero's cape.

Their inspiration comes from the supplies at hand. Rather than fret about what they do not have, they draw inspiration from what they do have.

We, as adults and leaders, should seek to remain connected to the childlike attitude which allows inspiration to flourish. Growing up does not mean we must lose the wonder of life.

Sources of Inspiration

For inspiration to work well, it has to be nourished. You can nourish your inspirational stockpile from a number of sources. Like tributaries feeding into a major river, these sources will help your inspiration flow ever stronger.

Collect things

Things which make you smile, make you happy, exercise your brain, and make you think all help to spark ideas, and make you want to keep going. The format may be a physical item, an image of an item or notes about an item. Collect them in whatever form works for you.

I happen to love books, flowers, all things nautical, puffins and zebras. So, I surround myself with the things which make me happy and bring a smile to my face. I collect photos of the things I love. I collect figurines and stuffed animals. I decorate with silk and living flowers. This bookshelf, just behind the desk in my office, brings me lots of inspiration each time I enter the room.

Some of the books in my collection are ones I have read and loved too much to let go. Some of the books talk about the things I love. Reference books in my collection help me grow in my craft. And some of the books, I am proud to say, are ones I have written or to which I have contributed.

If you have ever watched "The Ray Bradbury Theater" or visited the Center for Ray Bradbury Studies at Indiana University, you have seen one of my heroes as he worked when he was alive. Ray Bradbury's office held memorabilia and notes accumulated during his decades of living.[iii] Photos, statues, framed correspondence, miniatures, giant stuffed creatures, typewriters, awards and books, books, books! As he said in one version of the opening credits for his television series, he could not possibly go hungry for ideas in this environment.

Some industries call this dream building, a way to keep your goals and dreams firmly before you. Some label the process positive reinforcement. The label you hang on it is less important than accessing the process itself.

Collect memories of your successes, reminders of your goals and encouragement for the rough spots. And there will be rough spots, times when your brain is too tired to see the next step. The recollections of successes will help you to recover from those stalls and keep going.

Another thought about encouragement: it can be *about* you or it can be something which speaks *to* you.

A note from a reader of "Well done! I loved the book," or from your boss or co-worker of "Great job on that project" is encouragement about you. Keep those "Way to go!" notes for the days when you feel as though you have failed. They can remind you of the taste of success and keep you on track.

Outside encouragement may come from stories of overcomers, inspirational quotes or any other source where you can draw strength from another's success. Look at their pattern and adapt it to your own needs.

One of my "refuse to part with" books is a battered 1946 Readers Digest anthology I grew up with and inherited from my mother, entitled *Getting the Most Out of Life*. Cover to cover, it gives me hope and joy. I am a huge fan of the Chicken Soup for the Soul® series, too. Such books remind me to keep going.

Few climbers reach the summit of their target mountain without preparation, tools and a support team. Your collection contains all those elements for your inspiration. Even on those days when there is not anyone around to cheer you on, your collection will help.

The view from the mountaintop of your creativity will take your breath away. Do not be afraid to make the climb. The reward is worth the effort.

List a few of the things you have collected which inspire you:

_____

_____

_____

_____

_____

Photograph places, people and things.

Whether you are talking about places you have been, people you have met, or things you have seen, take plenty of photographs along the way. Use those photographs to remind you of what you have achieved, what you want to achieve and what you are doing to achieve it.

This photo was one of many I took while on the Hattiesburg Daylily Driving Tour several years ago. Daylily breeders across the region, members of the Hattiesburg Area Daylily Society,[iv] open their gardens for public viewing over a spring weekend. We drove from one beautiful location to another during a full day of fellowship and flowers.

The picture became, along with its companions, the inspiration for my first novel, *Death in the Daylilies*. The photographs became my reference materials as well as my inspiration. One of them even became the book's cover image.

A photo I took in Alaska surprised me when I had the pictures developed. (I took this back in the days of film, before digital cameras and smart phones.)

We had taken a ride on The White Pass & Yukon Route Railroad, a scenic railway out of Skagway. Instead of just the few impressive boulders along a wild river gorge I hoped I had captured, I had a stunning image which included soaring mountains and towering trees. The photo never fails to transport me back to the narrow-gauge train ride and a delightful excursion along the Yukon River to the U.S.-Canada border. I treasure the photo and the memory of a cherished trip with my family.

List some of the photographs which inspire you. Do you see a pattern in them?

_____
_____
_____
_____
_____

Copy things

This is a secret I learned from art students.

They copy the works of the great masters, not as an attempt to forge the work and fool someone, but as an exercise designed to help them understand the skills and techniques which go into creating a masterpiece. They learn image balance, develop an eye for detail and investigate a myriad of techniques.

Visit any art museum and you will likely see art students bent over their sketchbooks, learning by doing. "The practice of copying masterpieces has been one of the cornerstones of traditional art education for a long time."[v]

In 2015, the Rijksmuseum in Amsterdam in the Netherlands instituted a program called #startdrawing. As Wim Pijbes, the museum's general director, explains, "In our busy lives we don't always realize how beautiful something can be. We forget how to look really closely. Drawing helps because you see more when you draw. People who want to draw are always welcome in the Rijksmuseum."[vi]

As a teenager, I fell in love with poetry. Since I could not afford to purchase copies of all of the books containing my favorites, I started collecting them in a spiral bound notebook, handwritten. As I copied those great poems over the years, I learned more about the rhythm of a poem, rhyme schemes, subjects and poetic forms. All of these elements demonstrated themselves in the notebook. The poems I copied inspired me to learn more about writing poetry. When I write a poem today, I have all those poets of the past to thank for the lessons.

Sometimes, I write out a particularly beautiful or powerful prose passage from a book I am reading. This practice helps me get closer to the words, so I can better create my own passages with impact. The smooth coursing of a pen across paper reinforces the author's impact on me and activates my own creativity. Learning the patterns of excellent phrases hones my own skills and inspires me. Keeping the copies of them close reminds me of the target of excellence those authors have set for me.

My late paternal grandmother crocheted, and she crocheted beautifully. She could not follow a written pattern for anything, but she could look at someone else's finished piece and copy it to perfection. Once she got the stitch placement of a particular motif in mind, she could branch out and create her own patterns for everything from delicate doilies to lace collars for dresses and snuggly afghans. She copied to learn to create.

None of these copying techniques are meant to condone plagiarism or forgery, but rather to help school the learner in the tools of a discipline.

Copy those who have achieved what you want to achieve, so you can learn from the steps to success they have laid out for you. You will nourish your creative soul with positive lessons.

What are some of the things which you can copy as a learning tool?

_____

_____

_____

_____

_____

Study things

No one of us knows everything there is to know. By employing lifelong study, you not only feed your creativity, you also keep yourself young.

As a writer, I study writing techniques, genre descriptions, specific topics which apply to my books, psychology, criminology and more. I read the books of writers I admire and analyze why I admire them. If an opportunity to attend a webinar pops up when I am available, I grab it.

For *Death in the Daylilies*, I studied daylily growers and their techniques, the propagation methods applicable to daylilies, and other aspects of the culture. I talked with growers and breeders. I even bought a few cultivars for myself. I did not know much about them when I started, but I learned. The more I learned, the more I appreciated those who grow these beautiful flowers and the more their work inspired me.

Studying a new topic can energize your creativity. Learning invigorates the mind which in turn feeds inspiration.

What fields of interest would you like to study?

Listen to inspiring music

What sort of music lifts you? Is it a single musical form or a variety of them? Listen to those pieces which make you feel empowered, uplifted, filled with joy.

When I was a teenager, some of the people I knew would collect a hand-selected group of recordings onto a cassette and call it a "mix tape." Nowadays, people set up a playlist on an electronic device. The medium has changed but the idea is the same: choose the music you love. The name of the method is less important than the musical choices. Set up your own playlist of music which motivates, inspires and invigorates you.

Do not let anyone tell you what you *must* listen to for inspiration. Choose the music which inspires you, regardless of the format. My own list includes selections from classical, gospel, traditional jazz, show tunes, soul, rock and roll and country. Some come with lyrics while others are instrumentals. Each of them speaks to me in its own way. Each of them offers me a mental or emotional boost.

The most important feature of your choices should be how they make you feel. My favorites may not help you at all and your favorites may not work for me. No problem. Your choices are right for you and nothing else matters.

What music lifts you and inspires you?

_____

_____

Imagination

Imagination, coming up with new ideas, forms the backbone of creativity. Envision a new way to approach a problem by bringing previous knowledge together in a new way and you have called on your imagination.

As a society, we value imagination. We celebrate "imaginative" productions and solutions. When technology and imagination meet, we applaud "imagineering," a word coined by Alcoa Aluminum and trademarked by Walt Disney Corporation.[vii] Your own imagination is every bit as valuable.

Where do we get the imaginative ideas from which we can create? Curiosity is key. A sense of "I wonder" about something, a desire to know a little more about a topic or situation starts the process. The same curiosity behind the popularity of "reality" programming or the desire to head toward a siren pushes imagination and, in turn, creativity.

Who, what, where, when, how and why questions can provide powerful insights. Imagination takes over from there.

Begin by letting your thoughts run in a multitude of directions from the task at hand. Call it brainstorming, thought mapping or any other label you choose. Let ideas and images come, and then build on them.

Once more, take a look at children. I see this creative brainstorming demonstrated very clearly when I participate in a children's library program. We start out with a simple idea, like a figure made from toilet paper rolls covered in aluminum foil or construction paper. By the end of the session, we end up with an incredible variety of creations, all sprung from the minds of the participating children. Robots, doctors, dolls and more appear from the fertile fields of juvenile imaginations watered with an array of supplies.

In workshops with puppeteer Laura Anne Ewald of The Everyman Puppet Theatre,[viii] I have watched a single sheet of paper or a paper plate transform into fanciful puppets of intricate design. Children use nothing more than paper, glue and crayons or markers to bring their creations to life.

The children are not hindered by what is expected or what reality says. They cut loose with a big dose of "What can I make next?" Imagination, fueled by whatever supplies are at hand, burns brightly to light the way to creative play.

Here are some ways to power up your imagination, but do not feel limited to these. Add whatever methods you have found work for you from past experience. Glean ideas from others, as well. As a group of individuals pooling our strengths, we have far more resources than any one person alone.

Read

Read everything you can get your hands on which interests you or catches your eye. You never know what will spark your imagination. Fiction or nonfiction, historical or contemporary, book or periodical, any genre at all will offer fuel to your imagination's engine.

An online article about the identification of a new species of turtle in my area gave me the basis for one of my series of children's books. "Pearl the Turtle" was inspired by *Graptemys pearlensis*, the Pearl River map turtle, an endangered species indigenous to the Pearl River and its tributaries in Mississippi and Louisiana. The first story, *Pearl's Pool*, dealt with peer pressure, thinking for yourself and knowing when you have all you need.

Pearl's *persona* later came together with a situation I encountered on a quiet country road. I spotted a box turtle poised on the edge of the road as though about to cross. I stopped my car and moved the beautiful amphibian to the other side of the road in an attempt to prevent it from being run over by an inattentive driver.

The two turtles met in the second Pearl the Turtle book, *Pearl Makes a Friend*, and explored the idea of becoming friends with someone who does not look like you. Even plush turtles can be new friends.

When you take in information on a wide array of topics from a variety of sources, your mind can start to process the data in new ways. Like some sort of buffet restaurant menu, your brain can take a little something from one tray, something from a second bin and top it with a big something from another display. You have prepared a meal to feed your imagination and it will respond with a banquet of ideas.

Creativity

Where do you find assorted information to read?

_____
_____
_____
_____
_____

Visit

Get out of your everyday space. Visit a place you have not been before, maybe normally would not have even thought of going. I always find museums geared to children get my imagination going. Kids tend to look at the world through a lens of "everything is possible." When you spend time around them in a rich environment, you will start looking at things in the same way.

How about a historic or nature site in your area which you have skipped in the past? Those docents can fill your head with fascinating tidbits on the subject to spark your imagination. Some obscure detail can be just the prompt you need to get your ideas working.

Old solutions can be adapted and updated to address current situations. Ideas from the past can lead the way to newer ideas and innovations.

I love hanging out in nature preserves and arboretums. While walking a trail through The Crosby Arboretum in Picayune, MS, I was struck by how isolated some areas were. A crime could take place there unwitnessed! And so was born *Ambush at the Arboretum*, my second novel.

Another location I visited in the past which I plan to use is the Tea Room at JD Farms[ix]. The blueberry and tea farm just outside of town offers tea tasting in a dining room-like setting which set me to imagining a formal tea party showdown *a la* Agatha Christie for my current work-in-progress, *Blood on the Bottletree*.

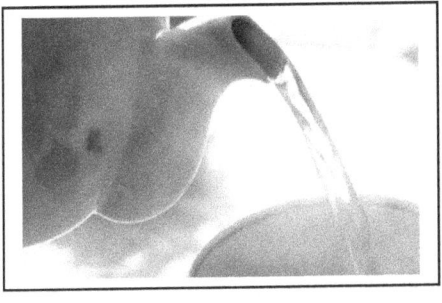

The setting, rich in the aromas of tea blends and the charm of a variety of tea services, speaks to me of intrigue and tradition, perfect for a tasteful showdown. And who knew Mississippi could grow tea?

Something as simple as a restaurant or coffeehouse can get the creative juices flowing. Listen to the conversations of fellow diners (discreetly, of course) and make notes of interesting comments, descriptions, names or anything else which captures your attention. Once the information percolates through your own worldview, you will have all sorts of imaginative ways to go.

List some places you'd like to visit for inspiration:

_____
_____
_____
_____
_____

Attend

Look for cultural and educational events to attend. Your public library or community college probably holds lectures on topics which interest you. The cost will be reasonable (maybe even free) and the rewards great. Events about arts, science and history can lead to leaps in other realms and *vice versa*, so do not discount any interesting topic.

Visit collections such as natural history museums, historic sites, reconstructed locales, vocational history museums and even oddball places.

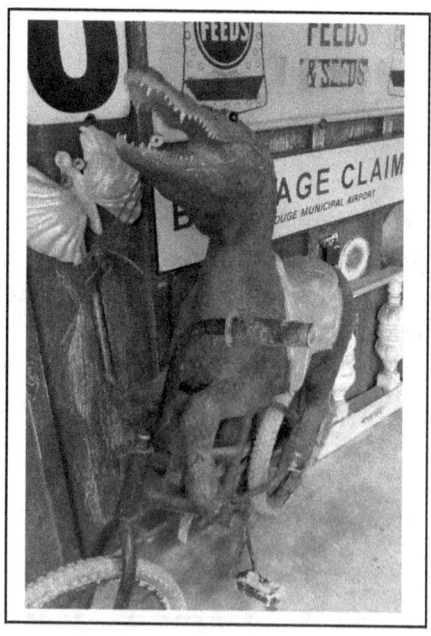

This bizarre creature, a combination of alligator and carousel pony, is part of the Abita Mystery House,[x] (also known as the UCM Museum) in Abita Springs, LA. An eclectic folk art museum, the Mystery House offers many strange sorts of "artifacts," including a huge collection of paint-by-number works, craft stick sculptures and other amazing oddities. Your imagination cannot help but feed on the outlandish exhibits there.

Another such delight exists in Hattiesburg, MS as Hattiesburg Pocket Museum.[xi] Hidden down a side alley in downtown, the museum brings unusual displays o a plethora of subjects. The exhibits change on a regular basis, offering a continually fresh source for fueling the imagination.

Does your company or business offer conferences, seminars or other collaborative events? Take advantage of them to hear new ideas, new combinations, data on projects and more. Some seemingly minor fact might be the spark which sends your imagination into overdrive.

Meet with others who share your interests. You will help each other stay up with the latest developments and can share insights to help each other grow. Create your own "think tank" in your field of interest.

List several events you'd like to attend:

_____
_____
_____
_____
_____

Borrow from the Arts

Learning about other expressive media can help your own expressive work improve. Art forms can feed on each other.

Ekphrastic poetry is a form which yields a poem based on a physical work of art. The original work may be a painting or sculpture, some sort of needlework or other visual art. The poet finds a way to express in words the feelings triggered by the artwork.

Writing competitions often ask for stories based on a particular image. Artists create images which depict a particular scene in a story. A song inspires a movie script. A book sparks an image for a painter. The circle goes on as the arts intertwine to strengthen each other.

You do not have to be a writer to try this creative exercise. Write a brief impression of this piece of sculpture.

Poetry or prose, fact or fiction, your choice. What do you see, feel or think when you look at Antoine Bourdelle's sculpture Hercules the Archer?[xii]

Imagine yourself meeting this fellow at a sporting event, encountering him on a hunt, being introduced at a party. Let the thoughts and ideas flow freely. Whether you approach your piece as an interview, a product ad, a fictional story or something else altogether, you will find your creativity firing on all pistons. I took this photograph of the statue in the Sydney and Walda Besthoff Sculpture Garden at the New Orleans Museum of Art in City Park, New Orleans, LA. The statue formerly stood in front of the museum (always one of my favorite landmarks when I was a child). Now it shares a vast area with a delightful collection of other sculptures in the park, outdoors just beyond the museum building. A visit to the garden allows one to enjoy nature and art at the same time.

List some pieces of art (in any media) which spark your imagination:

_____
_____
_____
_____
_____

Observe

Pay attention to what is going on around you. Look with a dedicated eye to pull in the details, large and small, which can help you fuel your imagination.

The human brain seems to be hardwired to look for patterns and connections[xiii] in the world around us. The details we perceive can contribute to our pattern recognition, but we have to make the effort to be aware of the details. Once we perceive the stimulus of a particular shape, sound or aroma, our creative mind will make associations and spark ideas.

When was the last time you watched the clouds with an eye toward something other than the weather? There are rich fields for imagination, ready for harvest, in the ever-shifting shapes and shadows of the clouds. For instance, what do you see in this cloud photo?

Give yourself a chance to really look skyward sometime soon. You may find fanciful creatures, historical figures, impressive buildings or more. And everything you see is stoking your imagination. Far from wasting time, cloud watching is an imagination-building activity.

Observe with all your senses. They set the stage for your perception of the world. When you employ them to gather the details of your surroundings, you give your imagination free rein.

Here is an exercise for you on using your senses. Close your eyes to avoid distraction by what you see. Concentrate on your surroundings. You may want to have someone read the questions to you one by one to allow you to respond without interruption.

a. What do you hear? Is it what you expected to hear? If not, what expected sound or sounds are absent? What unexpected sounds are present? What do they tell you about your environment?

b. What do you feel? Is the air cool or warm? Is the air moving around you or still? Do you sense dampness or dryness?

c. What do you smell? Scientists tell us a sense of smell is closely linked to our memory and emotions.[xiv] What aromas do you identify in your current environment? What do they say to you? What feelings and thoughts do they kindle?

d. What do you taste?[xv] Inhale through your opened mouth and concentrate on the sensations you feel on your tongue. Are they pleasant or unpleasant? How do you feel about the taste? What does it bring to mind?

e. Now open your eyes. What do you see? Did your senses prepare you for what you are viewing or was there a surprise? Did you notice something you had previously overlooked? How do you feel about the outcome?

Make notes about the senses you experienced. How do they help you to understand the world around you? How can you use them to enhance your creativity and apply them to your current situation?

All of our senses play into our perception of the world and our interactions with it. There is a reason why grocery stores send the aroma of freshly baked bread out into the store, why advertisers choose particular colors, why call systems choose particular "wait" music.

When we tune into our sensory input, we turn on new possibilities for solving our problem, answering our question, or revitalizing our creativity.

List some interesting things you have observed which got your imagination operating:

_____
_____
_____
_____
_____

Play a game

Game playing allows us to explore possibilities without boundaries. I am talking about logic games, puzzles, word games, jigsaw puzzles and such. The time you spend playing games can refresh your mind and in turn, your creativity.[xvi]

One game, guaranteed to provoke fun and imagination, is creating crazy acronyms. Start with the letters and create the title to go along. (Admit it, you have wondered about all those governmental agency and project acronyms, haven't you?)

Many years ago, I belonged to a local writers group focused on writing science fiction. The official name of the group began as the South Mississippi Professional Science Fiction Writers Association. The pretentious and overly long moniker did not last.

One of the members suggested we just call ourselves "SMART" because we were all intelligent enough to appreciate science fiction. A little pompous, perhaps, but it paved the way to what eventually became our permanent name – South Mississippi Armadillo Racing Team.

The fanciful title lent itself to all sorts of imaginative scenarios. Were we humans who raced armadillos? Armadillos who drove race cars? Race car drivers who kept armadillos as pets? Was the racing taking place on Earth or somewhere else?

Perhaps you can even see my favorite description: we were writers with tough enough shells to ward off negative reviews, and we could roll up to our typewriters (I know, I am dating myself here) to tell our stories.

Play can take many forms. Physical play, a rousing game of your favorite sport, can go a long way to rejuvenate your creativity. The increased blood flow and endorphin production will help you physically and mentally.

My granddaughter (who is six years old as I write this) and I play hide-and-seek regularly. She lives 900 miles away, so we play virtually. She moves off camera while I count, then I start my seeking.

"I wonder if she went into the garage." I tap-tap-tap on the desktop as I "walk" to the garage. And on I go, tapping my way through the rooms of the house: laundry room, upstairs to the bedrooms, down to the basement playroom, back up to the living room, into the kitchen, over to the patio door to check the backyard, and so on.

She giggles hysterically as I miss my guess, then pops back into view when I "find" her in her chosen hiding place. She gets to imagine me walking through her house, I get to imagine where she might have chosen to hide this time and we have a great time. Distance may separate us, but imagination brings us together through the medium of play.

Scientists are digging deeper into the role of play in wellbeing.[xvii] Even a rousing game of Solitaire can let your mind work on a different level than usual and free your creative thoughts. By changing mental gears, you give yourself a chance to see the world from a fresh perspective.

What games do you play for mental refreshment and imagination building?

"What If?" the Situation

Long a tool of speculative fiction authors, "What if?" offers limitless ways for your imagination to bloom. From alien worlds across the universe to alternative history here on earth, "What if?" can change a writer's perspective. The same question can help in whatever situation you are facing, as the 2020 COVID-19 pandemic proved.

Just take a look at these examples. What if…

- Teachers made the switch to video classes online?
- Public libraries began offering children's story time sessions online?
- Churches offered video services through social media?
- Garment companies began manufacturing masks and medical gowns instead of fashionable attire?
- Breweries and distilleries bottled hand sanitizer instead of alcoholic beverages?
- Restaurants and stores offered curbside pickup when patrons could not come inside?
- Ride share companies branched out into food delivery service?
- Musicians played concerts through video sharing applications or performed in small groups from balconies or rooftops?
- Rival drug companies joined forces to increase vaccine production?

Those businesses and services and many more used the "what if" scenario to find ways to keep going. Check out

YouTube for additional examples of how people coped with the changes brought about by this horrible pandemic.

Instead of "I can't do *whatever it is*," start with "What if I can?" From there, go on to "what if?" your way to possible solutions to help you accomplish the goal. Here are a few examples:

   a) **What if** the budget was not an issue in our planning decision? What options would we be free to consider?
   b) **What if** we switched the production line to a modified product? How would the change impact our customer base?
   c) **What if** we changed our hours and were open earlier? Later? Different days?
   d) **What if** we opened an online branch of the company?
   e) **What if** we worked with the local organization for challenged individuals to offer jobs in our company?
   f) **What if** we partnered with a complementary local company to offer more services through a single contact point?
   g) **What if** we invited high school seniors into our business plant/shop/store/kitchen to see how we work and show them potential job opportunities?
   h) **What if** we started a mentoring program in our community to match at-risk kids with retired seniors?
   i) **What if** we partnered local government to connect volunteers with needed community tasks

to help fill the voids left by lowered tax income and accompanying budget cuts?

Do not be afraid to pummel whatever your current problem is with as many "What if" questions as it takes to get past the feeling of "I can't" and move on to "I can." You will find "What if" questions to be one of the most creative tools in your imagination toolbox. Take them out on a regular basis and put them to use.

List some "What If" questions to help your problem-solving:

_____
_____
_____
_____
_____

Laugh often.

The Biblical prescription for laughter (Proverbs 17:22) still holds. Psychologists examine the link between creativity and laughter as a common theme. While enhancing creativity does not require you to become a stand-up comic, understanding how those presenters work can help you take the next step toward sparks and fireworks of your own.

> "Surprise is at the heart of comedy. Surprise is also at the heart of *creativity*. Creativity is about more than just producing something. It's about producing something in a new way, a different way, a surprising way. So, if you want to be creative in your life or work, it's important to be available to surprise."[xviii]

One handy tool is a laughter journal. Keep notes about events and situations which made you laugh. Review those entries when you feel stuck in a rut to help kick you into gear.[xix] Whether a joke, a silly mishap or a serendipitous event, a revisited laugh can bring you out of the doldrums.

Remember the alligator-carousel horse sculpture you saw earlier? Off-beat folk art museums like the Abita Mystery House serve up laughter in big quantities, so indulge your appetite for joy often.

Creativity

How does humor help? There are several channels at work. The distraction from thinking about a problem, relaxing for a moment, stretching your creative muscles—all of these and more are ways humor stimulates creativity.[xx]

Just as play can help free you from the everyday routine, so can humor. From the corniest "Knock, Knock" joke to the most sophisticated comedy routine, laughter is beneficial to your creative flow. Take a moment for a smile just for you:

> Knock, Knock
> > *(Who's there)*
> Plum
> > *(Plum who?)*
> Plumb brilliant, that's you!

List some things which make you laugh:

_____

_____

_____

_____

Information

We have already discussed the importance of taking in information from a variety of sources as it pertains to inspiration and imagination. Take a more in-depth look now at the basic process of garnering and using information.

Reading

Today's readers have more options than ever for accessing books. First and foremost, support your local library. Free access to books, past and present, helps to keep a society educated and informed.

Print media, electronic formats and audio books offer access to fit a variety of lifestyles. Most modern works come in multiple formats. Choose the one which works best for your situation.

Many other book resources are free; some are minimal cost. Check out some of these sources for older material. If you are researching the writings, science or culture of a past era, you will enjoy these sites, which provide access to out-of-print and public domain materials.

a) Project Gutenberg (https://www.gutenberg.org/). As of this writing, Project Gutenberg boasts more than free 60,000 titles. These are out-of-print books available in .pdf format. You can read them on the site or download them (often in a choice of electronic reader formats) to read later.
b) Open Library

(https://openlibrary.org/) Open Library claims to have more than three million titles available. One of those titles is my old friend, Getting the Most out of Life! (https://openlibrary.org/works/OL15160539W/Getting_the_most_out_of_life?edition=gettingmostoutof00plea)
c) Many Books (https://manybooks.net/). More than 50,000 titles.
d) International Children's Digital Library (http://en.childrenslibrary.org/). This site focuses on books for young readers in a variety of languages.

For more sites which share ebooks, search the internet for "free ebook." Before you click any links to sites, open a separate tab and check for reviews of the site to help avoid spam or hazardous sites.

Along the same vein as audio books, podcasts offer information on nearly any available topic to listeners via the internet. Search for podcasts on your subjects of interest and you can find programs to listen to while you exercise, work in the yard, commute or any other similar activity.

List your favorite resources for reading material:

_____
_____
_____
_____
_____

Experience your world

We have talked about visiting various locales as learning experiences, but do not forget to just take time to experience whatever is around you. From relationships to nature, emotions to physical events, your world will stimulate your imagination with input. The world you inhabit will inspire you with opportunities to grow and challenges to meet.

Let the everyday become special and the unusual become celebratory. For example, I am accustomed to anoles and geckos running around the porch, but the day I found my own little "dinosaur" is one I treasure. The magnificent fence swift was more than happy to pose for me and waited until I could get my cell phone out of my pocket. I consider such an event to be a serendipitous gift.

Look at the world from a perspective of "What new and wonderful thing is next?" and you will find special experiences all around you. Take a moment to appreciate them. Keep a record them for future enjoyment.

List some serendipitous moments in your life:

_____

_____

_____

_____

_____

Write it down

A journal or online note system can help you to organize all the pieces of information you have learned. Review your notes from time to time to give your brain the opportunity to integrate the ideas you have gleaned. Your subconscious can add the information to the store of knowledge at your disposal.

Have you seen the movie "Working Girl" with Harrison Ford and Melanie Griffith? When Griffith's character is challenged to explain how she came up with a particular business strategy, she pulls a conglomeration of seemingly unconnected articles and notes from her folder to show her process. Creativity at work!

The synthesis of information into inspiration through imagination requires some work on your part. If the information simply passes through your consciousness without making any impression, you will likely miss on creative opportunities. Take the time to let it make an impression.

Examine each source like a rare jewel. Hold it up to the light of your perception, turn it to see how the light strikes from different directions. Ask yourself, "How can I apply this to my life (or my problem)?" The more attentive time you spend with the information, the greater potential impact it can have.

If the source material is your own, use it as a repository for comments, questions and references. Highlighters and pens make great companions to your own books and notebooks.

If you do not own the source material, then make notes about the information. A three-ring binder, a journal, a spiral bound notebook or computerized word processing program can help you take and keep notes in an orderly manner. Be sure to document the original source so you can find it again if needed.

If you found the information online, be sure to record the web address for future reference. Try printing the page or saving as a .pdf for your records. While not every webpage allows for such use, many do.

Where do you keep records of inspirational and imaginative information?

_____
_____
_____
_____
_____

Record your idea fragments

Do not lose the benefit of your creativity. When the idea strikes, jot it down along with any relevant details. Be prepared for those odd moments of inspiration.

Here are a few tools to help:
a.) a small notebook and pen or pencil near your bed,
b.) a notes app or voice recording app on your mobile device,
c.) a washable grease pencil in the shower,
d.) an erasable whiteboard.

These temporary storage methods represent only a handful of the ways you can capture your ideas in the moment for later reference and preservation. Find the way or ways which work best for you and use them regularly.

At the earliest opportunity, transfer the idea to a more permanent storage method. Flesh out any additional details you have come up with and keep adding to the record over time until you are ready to implement the idea.

An idea allowed to escape is no use to you. An idea savored and saved can grow into creative solutions.

Where do you save your idea fragments?

Start Creating

Look into a mirror. Peering back at you is a creative mind in some field, whether you realize it or not.

My hope for you and your visit to this book is you *will* realize the creative potential you have inside and give it a chance to bloom. Once you tap into your creative self, your world will change for the better.

Creativity becomes a lifelong process of seeing possibilities and exploring avenues. Do not limit yourself to one approach. Be open to all the options ahead.

Go forth and be creative!

Appendix

The Creativity Bill of Rights

1. You have the God-given right to be creative.

2. You have the right to nurture your creativity.

3. You have the right to apply your creativity to a variety of situations and circumstances.

4. You have the right to appreciate the creative results of others.

5. You have the right to use curiosity as a divining rod to lead you toward creative discoveries in all realms of life.

6. You have the right to express your creativity in safe and productive ways which do no harm to others.

7. You have the right to use your creativity to make your life, your family, your work, your community, and your world a better place.

A Few Suggested Games

- Word games such as Scrabble, anagrams, crossword puzzles
- Rebus puzzles
- Sudoku puzzles
- Trivia games
- Jigsaw puzzles
- Problem-solving games such as mazes and matching games

Whether played online, in books or on tabletop boards, such games can enhance creativity.

Creativity Exercises

Here are a few exercises to get you started. Do not be afraid to create your own situations to continue.

- Imagine two historic characters from different eras, locations, or perspectives. For example, put Napoleon and Genghis Khan, Mother Teresa and Mao Zedong or Vincent Van Gogh and Albert Einstein in the same room. How would they interact? What would they talk about?
- Put a historic figure in a contemporary environment. How might he or she react? What questions would arise? What might seem unbelievable and what might seem a natural progression?
- Put a contemporary figure in a historic environment. What would the person miss most? What would be most appreciated about the period?
- Compare children's toys from the 1800s, 1900s and 2000s. What aspects have changed? What has remained the same?
- Examine the differences in food preparation between today and 200 years ago. What is better or healthier? What is less healthy or more difficult?
- What would happen if modern appliances stopped working? How would you cope with everyday tasks?
- Imagine yourself dropped in a foreign land. You have no local currency, you do not speak the language, you do not know the customs. What would you do to fit in? Would you ask for help or try to hide your vulnerability? Why?

Some Suggested Reading

These are a few of the books I turn to for encouragement and inspiration. Begin your own list and collection to keep you going.

Getting the Most out of Life: A Readers Digest Anthology

The Greatest Salesman in the World by Og Mandino

Chicken Soup for the Soul® series

The Places You'll Go by Dr. Seuss

The Power of Story series by Laura Anne Ewald

What other books come to mind?

_____

_____

_____

_____

_____

To Hercules

(On Antoine Bourdelle's *Hercules the Archer*)
by Mary Beth Magee

Noble sir, you've lost your garments.
Has your prey so stripped your pride?
Break your hunter's concentration
Long enough to go inside.

Put on trousers or a tunic,
Celtic kilt or Roman mail –
Anything, I beg you, archer,
For your undress leaves me pale.

Draw your bow in preparation,
Aim it high and set it loose.
Exact revenge against the thief
Who has exposed your bronze caboose.

Such disdain for social mores
May result in banishment.
Save your yourself by donning clothing,
Or stay hidden in your tent.

Hercules, I bow in wonder
At your muscles, strong and taut.
Now put your clothes on rippled sinew
Before a nasty cold you've caught.

© Mary Beth Magee

Photo Credits

Eat the Rainbow: Rezel Apacianado*

Sewing: Marília Castelli*

Tools: Jesse Orrico*

Bookshelf: Mary Beth Magee

Man with Red Backpack: Lucas Clara*

Daylily Garden: Mary Beth Magee

Alaska Landscape: Mary Beth Magee

Student: Santi Vedri*

Blanket Tent: Nathan Dumlao*

Pearl River Map Turtle: U.S. Geological Survey

Pearl and Becky: Mary Beth Magee

Arboretum Trail: Mary Beth Magee

Pouring Tea: Barrett Baxter

Hercules the Archer Sculpture: Mary Beth Magee

Gray Chick Cloud: Mary Beth Magee

Boxer with Punching Bag: Lorenzo Fattò Offidani*

Neon Laugh: Tim Mossholder*

Fence Swift Dragon: Mary Beth Magee

*   Photos courtesy www.unsplash.com

Books by Mary Beth Magee

Fiction

The (LOL)^4 Mysteries
Death in the Daylilies: Volume 1
Ambush at the Arboretum: Volume 2

The Cypress Point Chronicles
Volume 1: Cypress Point Confidences
Volume 2: A Cypress Point Christmas
Volume 3: Cypress Point Spirit

Journals

Devotions from the Road of Life Journal: A Caregiver's Medical Log
Getting Started in Your Own Kitchen: A Kitchen Planner and Cooking Journal for New Cooks
The Rose of Friendship: A Gratitude Journal
Get Started with Your Memoirs
The Storyteller's Journal

Nonfiction

Devotions from the Road of Life
Volume 1: Hitting the Road
Volume 2: Devotions for Caregivers
Volume 3: When the Road Gets Rough

Creativity: An Essential Tool for the Real World

Books for Children
Grandpa's Mustache
Pearl's Pool: Volume 1 of Pearl the Turtle
Pearl Makes a Friend: Volume 2 of Pearl the Turtle
Some More Cows
The Promise Wreath

Poetry
Songs of Childhood, Echoes of Years
Life and All: The Journey

Anthology Appearances
Chicken Soup for the Soul®: Thanks to My Mom
Chicken Soup for the Soul®: The Spirit of America
Chicken Soup for the Soul®: Believe in Miracles
Treasures Found in a Cedar Chest
Celebrating Mississippi (Mississippi Poetry Society South Branch)
Mississippi Poetry Journal 2018 Contest Edition
Southern Holidays (Mississippi Poetry Society South Branch)
Maps of the Heart
Inspire Promise
Inspire Hope
Not Your Mother's Book on Being a Parent
Not Your Mother's Book on Being a Stupid Kid

Connect with Mary Beth Magee

Website: www.LOL4.net

Email: info@botr.com

Facebook: MaryBethMageeWrites

Twitter: MaryBethWrites

Etsy: https://www.etsy.com/shop/BOTRPress/

Café Press: http://www.cafepress.com/profile/121587126

Where to Find Books by Mary Beth Magee

Order through your local bookstore (they can order it if they do not currently carry it).

Order on the web through:

      Amazon.com

      Audible.com

      Barnes & Noble

      Books-A-Million

      www.LOL4.net for autographed copies

If you already have a copy of one or more of her books and would like an autographed bookplate for it, email her with your snail mail address and how many you need. She will get them off to you. And thank you!

End Notes

[i] "Creativity." *Merriam Webster*, Merriam Webster, www.merriam-webster.com/dictionary/creativity. Accessed 6 Oct. 2020.

[ii] Khalil, Radwa, et al. "The Link Between Creativity, Cognition, and Creative Drives and Underlying Neural Mechanisms." *Frontiers in Neural Circuits*, vol. 13, no. 1, 2019, pp. 1–16. *Frontiers*, doi:10.3389/fncir.2019.00018/full.

[iii] *IUPUI*. bradbury.iupui.edu/pages/bradburys-office/index.php. Accessed 6 Oct. 2020.

[iv] *The Hattiesburg Area Daylily Society*. www.hattiesburgdaylily.com. Accessed 4 Oct. 2020.

[v] Nelson, Connie. "Copy a Painting by an Old Master: Improve Your Art at the Museum." *Explore-Drawing-and-Painting.Com/*, 2019, www.explore-drawing-and-painting.com/copy-painting-in-museum.html.

[vi] "Through the Rijksmuseum With a Pencil." *Rijksmuseum*, www.rijksmuseum.nl/en/press/press-releases/through-the-rijksmuseum-with-a-pencil. Accessed 28 Sept. 2020.

[vii] "The Place They Do Imagineering." *Alcoa Aluminum*, graphic-design.tjs-labs.com/show-picture?id=1118935951&size=FULL. Accessed 6 Sept. 2020.

[viii] Ewald, Laura Anne. "The Everyman Puppet Theatre." *YouTube*, Laura Anne Ewald, 13 Mar. 2020, www.youtube.com/channel/UCkYObjlEJYk4pQljkElXqZw.

[ix] "JD Farms." *Https://Jdfarms.Us/*, jdfarms.us. Accessed 5 Nov. 2020.

[x] *Abita Mystery House and the UCM Museum in Abita Springs Louisiana*. abitamysteryhouse.com. Accessed 9 Jan. 2021.

[xi] *Hattiesburg Pocket Museum*. Hattiesburg Convention Commission, hattiesburgconventioncommission.com/hattiesburg-pocket-museum. Accessed 21 Mar. 2021.

[xii] NOMA. "Hercules the Archer." *New Orleans Museum of Art*, 4 June 2020, noma.org/collection/hercules-the-archer.

[xiii] Ohio State University. "This is your brain detecting patterns: It is different from other kinds of learning, study shows." ScienceDaily. ScienceDaily, 31 May 2018.

[xiv] "Psychology and Smell." *Fifth Sense*, www.fifthsense.org.uk/psychology-and-smell. Accessed 5 Jan. 2021.

[xv] "The Science of Taste & Nutrition –." *Kerry Health And Nutrition Institute*, khni.kerry.com/taste/the-science-of-taste-nutrition/#:%7E: Accessed 10 Jan. 2021.

[xvi] Forman, Michael. "The Importance of Play in Adulthood." *Wanderlust*, 18 Sept. 2018, wanderlust.com/journal/the-importance-of-play-in-adulthood/#:%7E:

[xvii] "The Science." *National Institute for Play*, 5 Nov. 2020, www.nifplay.org/science/overview.

[xviii] Evans, David. "Laugh Your Way to Creativity." *Psychology Today*, 8 Nov. 2017, www.psychologytoday.com/us/blog/can-t-we-all-just-get-along/201711/laugh-your-way-creativity.

[xix] Maxine. "Laughter Fuels Creativity." *Creative You Learning Lab*, 3 June 2020, www.creativeyoulearninglab.com/laughter-fuels-creativity./

[xx] "Does Laughing Promote Creativity? – Psych2Go." *Psych2go.Net*, psych2go.net/laughing-promotes-creativity. Accessed 3 Oct. 2020.